UNLEASH YOUR HUSTLE: A STEP-BY-STEP GUIDE TO STARTING AND GROWING YOUR ONLINE BUSINESS

First edition. February 22, 2024.

ISBN: 979-8224323609

Written by Brandon Allen.

Table of Contents

Unleash Your Hustle: A Step-by-Step Guide to Starting and Growing Your Online Business

Brandon Allen

Introduction

In an era where the digital landscape is continuously evolving, the dream of starting your own online business has never been more accessible or enticing. The internet has democratized entrepreneurship, offering limitless opportunities to those willing to seize them. Yet, the path to success can seem overwhelming with so much information available. That is where "Unleash Your Hustle" comes in.

This book is more than just a guide; it is a roadmap to transforming your ambition into action. Whether you are dreaming of turning your passion into profit or scaling your side hustle into a full-time venture, you are in the right place. We will navigate the journey of starting and growing your online business together through a blend of foundational principles, step-by-step strategies, and real-world insights.

Why focus on the hustle? Because in the world of online entrepreneurship, hustle is the bridge between ideas and reality. It is the relentless pursuit of your goals, armed with the right knowledge and tools. But make no mistake—this book is not about glorifying non-stop work at the expense of your well-being. Instead, it is about smart, strategic action that aligns with your vision and values.

We will begin by cultivating a mindset for success, recognizing that the right attitude is the bedrock of any thriving business. From there, we will dive into practical steps for finding your niche, planning your business, building your online presence, and much more. Each chapter is designed to move you closer to your goals, with actionable advice and exercises that turn learning into doing.

Throughout this journey, you will hear stories of individuals who have been where you are now and hustled their way to success. Their experiences will illuminate the challenges and triumphs of building an online business, offering lessons and inspiration to fuel your path.

So, are you ready to unleash your hustle? The road ahead is both exciting and challenging, but with this guide in hand, you are already one step closer to building the business of your dreams. Let us get started.

Chapter 1: Mindset For Success

I magine embarking on the most significant journey of your life with a map that has the power to dynamically update itself, ensuring you are always on the path to success, regardless of the obstacles you encounter. This map is not a physical one; it is the mindset you adopt as you navigate the entrepreneurial landscape. The right mindset can illuminate the path ahead, helping you to pivot, adapt, and grow even in the face of challenges. It is the difference between those who dream and those who do, between aspiring entrepreneurs and successful ones.

In this chapter, we will explore the foundational element of every successful entrepreneur's journey: the mindset. You will learn not just what it means to have a "Mindset for Success," but also how to cultivate it, nurture it, and employ it as your greatest asset in the quest to build and grow your online business.

Understanding Mindset

At its core, mindset represents our cognitive processes: our attitudes, beliefs, and ways of thinking about the world and ourselves. Researcher Carol Dweck, in her pioneering work, identifies two primary mindsets that significantly impact our lives and achievements: the fixed mindset and the growth mindset.

- **Fixed Mindset**: Individuals with a fixed mindset believe that their abilities, intelligence, and talents are static traits. They perceive challenges as threats, avoid risks, and prefer to stay within their comfort zone, leading to stagnation.
- **Growth Mindset**: In contrast, those with a growth mindset see abilities as malleable — something that can be developed and expanded through dedication, hard work, and perseverance. They embrace challenges, learn from criticism, and persist in the face of setbacks, viewing each as an opportunity to gain experience and learn.

The mindset you cultivate profoundly influences your entrepreneurial journey. A growth mindset is not just beneficial but essential in the dynamic, often unpredictable world of online business. It fuels resilience, encourages innovation, and fosters a culture of continuous improvement and learning.

Cultivating a Growth Mindset

Developing a growth mindset is a deliberate, intentional process that begins with recognizing and adjusting how you interpret challenges, setbacks, and criticism. Here are actionable strategies to start cultivating a growth mindset today:

1. **Embrace Challenges**: View each challenge as an opportunity to expand your skills and evaluate your limits. Instead of avoiding difficult tasks, approach them with curiosity and determination.
2. **Persist in the Face of Setbacks**: When faced with obstacles, take a step back to reassess and strategize rather than give up. Understand that every successful entrepreneur has encountered setbacks — what sets them apart is their willingness to persevere.
3. **See Effort as a Path to Mastery**: Recognize that effort is a necessary part of the journey toward excellence. Value hard work and dedication as essential components of success, not as mere means to an end.
4. **Learn from Criticism**: Use feedback as a tool for learning and self-improvement. Approach criticism with an open mind, identifying actionable insights that can help you grow.
5. **Find Lessons and Inspiration in the Success of Others**: Instead of feeling threatened by the success of others, look for lessons and inspiration. Understanding that success is achievable can motivate you to reach your own goals.

By incorporating these strategies into your daily life, you begin to shift your mindset from fixed to growth-oriented. This shift does not happen overnight, but with persistence and practice, it becomes part of who you are — an entrepreneur poised for success, equipped with the most powerful tool of all: a mindset geared for growth and achievement.

Overcoming Fear and Failure

Fear and failure are not only common but essential components of the entrepreneurial journey. Yet, their presence does not have to be a roadblock. Instead, they can be transformative forces that drive innovation, learning, and resilience.

Embracing Fear: The first step in overcoming fear is to acknowledge it. Fear, in its essence, is a protective mechanism — a signal from our brains that we are venturing into the unknown. Entrepreneurs face this regularly, whether while launching a new product, pitching to investors, or venturing into new markets. Embrace fear as a sign that you are pushing boundaries and growing. Analyze the root causes of your fears and address them systematically. Is the fear of failure holding you back because you are worried about financial security, or is it the fear of public judgment? By pinpointing the exact source, you can develop targeted strategies to confront and manage these fears.

Learning from Failure: Failure is an inevitable part of trying something new, which is a daily reality for entrepreneurs. The key to overcoming failure is not to avoid it but to learn from it. When faced with failure, conduct a post-mortem analysis. What went wrong? What could you have done differently? What did you learn? This approach transforms failure from a negative result into a valuable stepping stone towards success. Remember, many of the world's most successful entrepreneurs failed multiple times before finding success.

Cultivating Resilience: Resilience is the ability to bounce back from setbacks stronger than before. It is built through experience and practice.

Develop resilience by setting small, achievable challenges for yourself and gradually increasing their difficulty. Celebrate the wins, learn from the losses, and remind yourself of your progress and learning each step of the way. Building a support network of mentors, peers, and advisors can also provide encouragement and advice, making the journey less isolating and more manageable.

Setting Goals and Vision

Success in business, as in life, begins with setting clear, actionable goals. Goals give you a target to aim for, a direction to head in, and milestones to measure your progress.

Setting SMART Goals: SMART goals are Specific, Measurable, Achievable, Relevant, and Time-bound. They provide a clear framework for creating actionable objectives. For instance, instead of setting a vague goal like "increase sales," a SMART goal would be "increase sales by 20% within the next six months through online marketing and customer referral programs."

Vision Setting: While goals are about tangible achievements, vision is about the bigger picture. It is the driving force behind your goals, the ultimate image of what you want to achieve. Crafting a compelling vision involves imagining where you want your business to be in the future — think five, ten, or even twenty years ahead. What impact do you want to have on your customers, your community, or the world? Your vision should inspire and motivate you, providing a constant reminder of why you are doing what you are doing.

Aligning Actions with Vision: Once you have a vision, every action and goal should align with it. This ensures that your daily tasks contribute to your larger objectives. Regularly review your actions and goals to ensure they are in harmony with your vision. If they are not, it may be time to adjust your strategies or reassess your vision to reflect your current priorities and insights.

By combining a deep understanding of mindset with practical strategies for overcoming fear, learning from failure, and setting effective goals and visions, you lay the foundation for a successful entrepreneurial journey. These components are interconnected, each playing a vital role in shaping entrepreneurial experience. As you move forward, remember that mindset is not static; it is a dynamic attribute that evolves with experience and intention. Cultivating a positive, growth-oriented mindset is a continuous process — one that is central to achieving lasting business success.

The Power of Persistence

Persistence is often cited as one of the key factors behind the success of the world's leading entrepreneurs. It is the quality that allows you to continue moving forward, even when faced with seemingly insurmountable obstacles.

Understanding Persistence: At its core, persistence is the determination to keep going despite challenges and setbacks. It is about maintaining your drive and ambition, even when the path ahead is unclear or difficult. Persistence is not about blind perseverance but about maintaining your focus on your goals and vision and adapting your strategies as necessary.

Strategies for Building Persistence:

1. **Set Clear, Incremental Goals**: Breaking down your larger objectives into smaller, manageable tasks can make the journey seem less daunting and help maintain your momentum.
2. **Celebrate Small Wins**: Acknowledging and celebrating each small victory along the way can boost your morale and keep you motivated.
3. **Learn from Every Experience**: Instead of seeing setbacks as failures, view them as learning opportunities. This mindset shift can help you maintain your drive and find new ways to overcome challenges.
4. **Seek Support**: Having a network of peers, mentors, and supporters can provide encouragement, advice, and a fresh perspective when you are facing tough times.
5. **Remind Yourself of Your 'Why'**: Regularly revisiting the reasons behind your entrepreneurial journey can reignite your passion and perseverance.

Embracing Continuous Learning

In the fast-paced world of online business, continuous learning is not just an advantage; it is a necessity. The landscape is constantly evolving, and staying informed and adaptable is crucial for success.

The Importance of Lifelong Learning: Embracing a mindset of continuous learning allows you to stay ahead of industry trends, improve your skills, and innovate within your business. It is about being curious, seeking out new knowledge, and being open to change.

Ways to Incorporate Learning into Your Routine:

1. **Dedicate Time for Learning**: Set aside regular time in your schedule for reading, online courses, webinars, or other educational resources.
2. **Apply What You Learn**: Theoretical knowledge is valuable, but

applying what you learn to real-world scenarios is what truly drives growth.

3. **Learn from Others**: Engage with mentors, attend networking events, and collaborate with peers to gain diverse insights and knowledge.
4. **Reflect and Adapt**: After learning something new, reflect on how it applies to your business and how you can adapt your strategies accordingly.

Nurturing Emotional Intelligence

Emotional intelligence (EQ) is the ability to understand and manage your own emotions, as well as recognize and influence the emotions of others. In entrepreneurship, high EQ can lead to better decision-making, leadership, and relationships.

Components of Emotional Intelligence:

1. **Self-awareness**: Understanding your emotions, strengths, weaknesses, and values.
2. **Self-regulation**: Managing your emotions and impulses effectively.
3. **Motivation**: Harnessing your emotions to drive you towards your goals.
4. **Empathy**: Understanding and considering the feelings of others.
5. **Social Skills**: Building and managing relationships effectively.

Developing Your Emotional Intelligence:

1. **Practice Mindfulness**: Regular mindfulness or meditation can enhance your self-awareness and regulation.
2. **Seek Feedback**: Constructive feedback from others can provide insights into your emotional patterns and behaviors.
3. **Observe and Reflect**: Pay attention to your interactions and their outcomes. Reflect on what you did well and what you could improve.

4. **Empathize**: Try to see situations from others' perspectives, which can improve your empathy and social skills.

Developing a successful entrepreneurial mindset is a multi-faceted journey that encompasses cultivating a growth mindset, overcoming fear and failure, setting clear goals and visions, persisting through challenges, embracing continuous learning, and nurturing emotional intelligence. Each of these components plays a crucial role in shaping the kind of resilient, adaptable, and insightful entrepreneur who can navigate the difficulties of business with grace and tenacity.

Chapter 2: Finding Your Niche

Choosing the right niche is like setting the sails on your entrepreneurial journey. It determines the direction, speed, and destination of your online business voyage. A well-chosen niche allows you to focus your efforts, stand out in the market, and connect deeply with a specific audience. This chapter will guide you through the process of discovering your niche and combining your passions and skills with a marketable opportunity. By the end, you will be equipped to make an informed decision that aligns with your goals and sets you up for success.

Understanding What a Niche Is

In the vast ocean of the online market, a niche represents a specific, defined segment of the market that you choose to serve. It is more than just a product category or target demographic; it is a focused area where your specific interests, skills, and values intersect with customer needs and desires. Unlike a broad market, which can be crowded and highly competitive, a niche targets a specialized area, offering tailored solutions to a distinct audience.

The Benefits of Niche Marketing

Diving into a niche has several advantages that can significantly impact the success of your online business:

1. **Focused Target Audience**: By targeting a specific niche, you can create highly tailored marketing strategies that speak directly to the needs and desires of your audience, increasing engagement and conversion rates.
2. **Reduced Competition**: A well-defined niche helps you avoid the overcrowded general market, reducing the number of direct competitors and making it easier to stand out.
3. **Enhanced Customer Relationships**: Niche businesses can foster closer relationships with their customers, leading to higher levels of customer loyalty and word-of-mouth marketing.
4. **Increased Expertise and Authority**: Focusing on a niche allows

you to build deep knowledge and expertise, establishing your business as an authority in the area, which can attract more customers and opportunities.

Identifying Your Passions and Skills

The intersection of your passions and skills is where your ideal niche may lie. Begin by listing what you love to do, areas you are knowledgeable about, and skills you possess. Consider experiences that have shaped you, hobbies you cannot get enough of, and talents that others admire in you. The key is to find an overlap between what you are passionate about and what you are good at — and then match it to what the market needs.

Researching Your Niche

Deep Dive into Audience Needs

- Engage directly with potential customers through social media, forums, and in-person or virtual meetups. Look for recurring themes in their questions, complaints, and praises to understand their core needs.
- Conduct surveys or polls within these communities to gather quantitative data on preferences, needs, and gaps in the current market offerings.

Advanced Keyword Research

- Utilize keyword research tools to not only assess the search volume but also the intent behind the searches. Tools like AnswerThePublic can provide questions and prepositions associated with your keywords, giving deeper insights into what your target audience seeks.
- Analyze long-tail keywords to uncover niche-specific queries that indicate a high intent to purchase or engage.

Competitive Analysis Beyond the Surface

- Use tools like SEMrush or Ahrefs to conduct a competitive analysis that goes beyond what is visible on their websites. Look into their backlink profiles, organic search rankings, and paid advertising

strategies.
- Identify content gaps in your competitors' strategies. What questions are they not answering? What needs are they not addressing? This can reveal opportunities for differentiation.

Evaluating Niche Viability

Market Demand Exploration

- Leverage Google Trends to monitor the interest in your niche over time and predict its future direction. Pay special attention to seasonal variations or emerging trends that could impact demand.
- Utilize social listening tools like Brand24 or Mention to gauge the social media buzz around your niche. High levels of engagement and conversation can indicate a healthy interest.

In-depth Competition Analysis

- Evaluate not just the number of competitors but the quality of their offerings. Are there areas where they are consistently falling short? Customer reviews on platforms like Amazon, Yelp, or Trustpilot can provide valuable insights.
- Consider the barriers to entry in your niche. High barriers can be a double-edged sword, offering protection if you enter but making it harder to establish yourself initially.

Profitability Assessment

- Calculate potential profit margins by researching supplier costs, potential selling prices, and average market rates for similar products or services.
- Explore multiple revenue streams within your niche. For example, besides selling products, could you offer related services, online courses, or digital products to diversify your income?

Testing Your Niche Idea

Building and Utilizing an MVP

- Design your MVP to solve a core problem for your target audience. It does not need to have all the features of your final product but should deliver value and address the primary need.
- Collect feedback systematically through surveys, interviews, and usage data. Look for patterns in the feedback to guide further development.

Landing Page Optimization and Testing

- Use A/B testing on your landing pages to refine messaging, offers, and design elements based on conversion rates. Tools like Unbounce or Optimizely can simplify this process.
- Track the source of your traffic and conversions to understand which marketing channels are most effective for reaching your target audience.

Pilot Services and Feedback Loops

- When offering pilot services, set clear expectations with your early customers that their feedback is crucial to your development process. Offer incentives for detailed feedback.
- Implement a feedback loop where you regularly update these customers on how their input has influenced your service. This not only helps refine your offering but also builds customer loyalty.

Finalizing Your Niche Choice

Synthesizing Your Research and Test Results

- Gather all collected data and feedback into a detailed report to evaluate if your niche meets your criteria for market demand, competition, profitability, and compatibility with your interests and abilities.
- Conduct a SWOT analysis (Strengths, Weaknesses, Opportunities, Threats) to visualize where your potential niche stands in relation to the market and your capabilities.

Decision-making and Strategic Planning

- If research gives permission, start crafting detailed business and marketing plans for your niche. If findings are inconclusive, assess

whether tweaking your niche or strategy could resolve any issues.
- Remember, flexibility is key. The ability to pivot based on validated learning is a strength, not a setback. Be prepared to iterate on your niche choice as you gather more insights and the market evolves.

This thorough exploration of researching, evaluating, and testing your niche idea underscores the importance of a data-driven approach to niche selection. By meticulously following these steps, you ensure that your business idea is not only aligned with your passions and skills but is also viable and poised for success in the competitive online marketplace.

Chapter 3: Planning Your Business

Embarking on the entrepreneurial journey without a map can lead you into uncharted and often treacherous territory. A business plan acts as your guide, outlining the path from where you are now to where you want to be. It is not just a document for attracting investors but a strategic tool for clarifying your vision, setting goals, and detailing the steps needed to achieve them. This chapter will walk you through creating a comprehensive business plan tailored to your online business, ensuring you are prepared for the challenges and opportunities ahead.

The Purpose of a Business Plan

A business plan serves multiple purposes: it is a roadmap for your business, a tool to test your ideas, and, often, a requirement for securing funding. It forces you to think through all aspects of your business, from understanding your market to financial planning. Whether you are drafting a lean plan for internal use or a detailed document for investors, the goal is the same: to articulate your vision and the strategies you will employ to turn that vision into reality.

Defining Your Business Model

Your business model is the framework for how your business creates, delivers, and captures value. In the digital realm, this might mean selling physical goods through e-commerce, offering digital products, running a subscription service, or generating revenue through advertising. Choosing the right model depends on your niche, target audience, and personal goals. This section will explore popular online business models, providing insights to help you select the most suitable one for your venture.

Market Analysis

Understanding your market is crucial for the success of your business. This involves identifying your target audience, analyzing their needs and behaviors, and keeping abreast of market trends. Detailed market analysis informs product development, marketing strategies, and sales approaches, ensuring they resonate with your intended customers. We will guide you through conducting thorough market research, utilizing both primary and secondary sources, to build a solid foundation for your business decisions.

Competitive Analysis

In-depth Understanding of Your Competitors

Before you can confidently enter the market, it is crucial to know who you are up against. This means going beyond a surface-level understanding of your competitors.

1. **Identify Your Competitors**: Start with a broad list of businesses in your niche, then narrow it down to those that directly compete with your offering. Use tools like SimilarWeb and Alexa for online research, and do not overlook social media and forums where brands interact with their audience.

2. **Analyze Their Offerings**: Examine your competitors' products or services in detail. What features do they offer? What price points are they targeting? Understand their value proposition and how it resonates with their customers.

3. **Marketing Strategies**: Dive into their marketing tactics. Which channels are they active on? What kind of messaging do they use? Analyze their content strategy, SEO efforts, and social media presence. Tools like BuzzSumo and Ahrefs can provide insights into their most successful content and keywords.

4. **Customer Feedback**: Look for customer reviews on platforms like Trustpilot, Amazon, or even their own website. This can reveal what customers appreciate about their offerings and where they see room for improvement.

5. **SWOT Analysis**: Conduct a SWOT analysis (Strengths, Weaknesses, Opportunities, Threats) for each main competitor. This will help you identify opportunities where you can differentiate and threats you need to be aware of.

Marketing and Sales Strategy

Crafting a Winning Strategy

Your marketing and sales strategy is how you will attract and convert customers. It needs to be both comprehensive and flexible, tailored to your target audience and the realities of your market.

1. **Target Audience Definition**: Refine your understanding of your target audience. Create detailed buyer personas that include demographics, interests, and pain points. This will guide your marketing efforts and content creation.
2. **Marketing Channels**: Choose the marketing channels most effective for reaching your audience. Consider a mix of digital marketing tactics such as SEO, content marketing, social media, email marketing, and paid advertising. Each channel should have a clear goal and metrics for success.
3. **Content Strategy**: Develop a content strategy that addresses your audience's needs and interests at various stages of the buyer's journey. Plan your content calendar, considering blog posts, videos, podcasts, and social media content that educates, engages, and converts your audience.
4. **Sales Funnel**: Design your sales funnel with a clear path for converting leads into customers. This includes lead capture mechanisms, nurturing strategies (like email sequences), and conversion tactics (such as limited-time offers or demos).
5. **Measurement and Adjustment**: Establish KPIs for each marketing and sales activity. Use tools like Google Analytics, CRM software, and social media analytics to track performance. Be prepared to adjust your strategies based on what the data tells you.

Operations Plan

Setting Up for Smooth Operations

Your operations plan outlines how your business will run on a day-to-day basis. It covers everything from the production of goods or services to delivery to the customer.

1. **Key Operational Processes**: Map out the key processes needed to create and deliver your product or service. This includes supply chain management, production schedules, and delivery mechanisms.
2. **Technology and Tools**: Identify the technology and tools that will support your operations. This might include e-commerce platforms, project management software, customer service tools, and any industry-specific technologies.
3. **Suppliers and Partnerships**: For product-based businesses, detail your suppliers and any partnerships critical to your operations. For service-based businesses, outline any external contractors or services on which you will rely.
4. **Human Resources Plan**: Determine the roles and expertise needed to run your business effectively. Plan your hiring strategy, considering both full-time employees and freelancers or contractors.
5. **Risk Management**: Identify potential operational risks and how you'll mitigate them. This could include backup suppliers, data security measures, and insurance.

Financial Planning

Creating a Solid Financial Foundation

Financial planning within your business plan is crucial for defining your financial model, understanding startup costs, projecting revenue, and ensuring profitability. This section will guide you through the key components of financial planning for your online business.

1. **Startup Costs**: Begin by identifying all initial costs required to launch your business. This includes one-time expenses such as website development, purchasing domain names, initial inventory for product-based businesses, software subscriptions, and any necessary equipment. Use a spreadsheet to list and categorize these costs accurately.
2. **Operating Expenses**: Outline your ongoing operating expenses, which may include hosting fees, software subscriptions, marketing and advertising costs, salaries or freelancer fees, and office supplies. Understanding your burn rate, or how quickly you spend your capital, is essential for financial planning.
3. **Revenue Streams**: Clearly define how your business will make money. Will you sell products directly, offer services, use affiliate marketing, or rely on advertising revenue? Detail each revenue stream, including pricing strategies and expected conversion rates or sales volumes.
4. **Financial Projections**: Develop a set of financial projections, including profit and loss statements, cash flow forecasts, and balance sheets for at least the first three years. These projections should account for your startup costs, operating expenses, and expected revenue. Use conservative estimates for sales and revenue to ensure realism.
5. **Break-even Analysis**: Perform a break-even analysis to determine when your business will be able to cover all its expenses with its revenue. Knowing your break-even point is crucial for understanding the viability of your business model and setting realistic financial goals.
6. **Funding Requirements**: If you require external funding to start or grow your business, clearly specify the amount needed and how it will

be used. Detail any existing investments, loans, or grants and outline your plans for future funding rounds or revenue reinvestment.

7. **Financial Management Practices**: Describe the systems and practices you will use for managing your business finances, including accounting software, invoicing systems, and financial monitoring and reporting. Highlight how you will ensure compliance with tax laws and financial regulations.

8. **Risk Management and Contingencies**: Detail the financial management techniques and tools for your business, including accounting software, billing systems, and financial tracking and reporting. Explain how you will maintain adherence to tax and financial regulations.

Measuring Success

Setting and Tracking Key Performance Indicators (KPIs)

Beyond the initial financial plan, it's vital to establish metrics for ongoing monitoring and evaluation of your business's financial health.

1. **Key Performance Indicators**: Identify the critical KPIs relevant to your business model, such as customer acquisition cost (CAC), lifetime value (LTV) of a customer, gross margin, net profit margin, and cash flow. These indicators will help you measure the efficiency, profitability, and sustainability of your business.

2. **Regular Financial Reviews**: Schedule monthly or quarterly financial reviews to compare your actual performance against your projections. This practice will help you identify trends, adjust your budget, and make informed decisions to improve financial health and growth.

3. **Adjusting Your Plan**: Be prepared to adjust your financial plan based on performance data, market changes, and new opportunities. A flexible financial strategy allows you to pivot when necessary, capitalizing on new trends or technologies to enhance revenue and profitability.

Crafting a detailed and realistic financial plan is foundational to the success of your online business. It not only guides your initial launch and operational strategies but also provides a benchmark for measuring growth and identifying areas for improvement. By thoroughly planning your finances, regularly reviewing your performance, and being willing to adapt, you can build a financially stable and thriving business.

Chapter 4: Building Your Online Presence

I n the digital era, establishing a strong online presence is not just an option but
a necessity for businesses aiming to thrive and expand. Your online presence
is your digital storefront, the first point of contact many customers will have with
your brand. This chapter will guide you through the critical steps of building and
enhancing your online presence, from crafting a user-friendly website to
implementing a dynamic content strategy and engaging on social media. By the
end, you will have the tools and knowledge needed to make your business visible
and attractive to your target audience online.

Choosing the Right Website Platform

The foundation of your online presence is your website. Selecting the right
platform is crucial, as it impacts everything from the design and functionality of
your site to its maintenance and scalability.

- **Consider Your Needs**: Are you selling products directly online?
  Do you need a blog or a portfolio? Your business goals will dictate the
  features you need from a website platform.
- **Ease of Use**: Look for a platform that offers the right balance
  between customization and ease of use. Platforms like WordPress,
  Shopify, and Squarespace cater to different needs and skill levels.
- **Scalability**: Choose a platform that can grow with your business.
  Consider the costs of scaling up and the additional features you may
  need in the future.
- **Support and Community**: A platform with strong community
  support and readily available resources can be invaluable, especially if
  you are managing your site independently.

Creating a Compelling Website

Your website should not only reflect your brand but also be designed with your
target audience in mind.

- **Design and User Experience**: A clean, appealing design and intuitive navigation are essential. Users should find what they are looking for easily.

- **Mobile Responsiveness**: With more people accessing the Internet via mobile devices, ensure your site is mobile-friendly.
- **Clear Call to Action (CTA)**: Each page should guide visitors toward a specific action, whether it is making a purchase, signing up for a newsletter, or contacting you for more information.
- **Speed and Security**: Site speed affects user experience and SEO. Also, ensure your site is secure, especially if you are handling customer data.

Content Strategy for Your Online Presence

Crafting a Dynamic Content Strategy

Your content strategy is the backbone of your online presence, driving traffic to your website and engaging your audience.

- **Identify Your Audience's Needs**: Understand what information your audience is seeking. This could range from educational content, entertainment, or insights into your products or services.
- **Diversify Your Content**: Incorporate a mix of blog posts, videos, infographics, and podcasts to cater to different preferences and increase engagement.
- **Consistency is Key**: Regularly updating your website with fresh content keeps your audience coming back and helps improve your SEO ranking.
- **Measure and Adapt**: Use analytics to track the performance of your content. Which types are most popular? Adjust your strategy based on these insights to better meet your audience's needs.

Leveraging Social Media Effectively

Building Your Brand on Social Media

Social media platforms offer powerful channels to build your brand, connect with your audience, and drive traffic to your website.

- **Select the Right Platforms**: Not all social media platforms will be right for your business. Choose platforms where your target audience is most active and engaged.
- **Create Engaging Content**: Social media content should be engaging, shareable, and relevant to your audience. Use a mix of posts, including behind-the-scenes looks, product highlights, and interactive content like polls and quizzes.
- **Interact with Your Audience**: Social media is a two-way street. Respond to comments, messages, and mentions to build a community around your brand.
- **Schedule and Analyze**: Use scheduling tools to maintain a consistent presence. Analyze your social media metrics to understand what is working and refine your approach.

Search Engine Optimization (SEO)

Improving Your Website's Visibility

SEO is critical for making your website more visible to your target audience through search engines.

- **Keyword Research**: Identify keywords that your target audience uses to search for your products or services. Tools like Google Keyword Planner and Moz Keyword Explorer can help.
- **On-Page SEO**: Optimize your website's content and meta tags (title, descriptions, headings) with your target keywords. Ensure your website's structure and URLs are search engine friendly.
- **Off-Page SEO**: Build reputable backlinks to your website from other authoritative sites. Guest blogging and content marketing can help with this.
- **Technical SEO**: Ensure your website is technically optimized for SEO, including fast loading times, mobile optimization, and secure connections (HTTPS).

Email Marketing Integration

Nurturing Leads and Customers

Email marketing remains one of the most effective ways to nurture leads and maintain customer engagement.

- **Build Your Email List**: Offer incentives for website visitors to sign up for your mailing list, such as free e-books, webinars, or discount codes.
- **Segment Your Audience**: Tailor your emails to different segments of your audience based on their interests and behaviors for more personalized communication.

- **Deliver Value**: Your emails should provide value to your subscribers, whether through informative content, exclusive deals, or updates about your products or services.
- **Compliance and Optimization**: Ensure your email marketing practices comply with regulations like GDPR. Use A/B testing to optimize your email campaigns for higher open rates and engagement.

Monitoring and Analyzing Your Online Presence

Tracking Success and Making Informed Adjustments

To ensure your online presence is effectively contributing to your business goals, it is vital to monitor and analyze your efforts across all platforms.

- **Web Analytics**: Utilize tools like Google Analytics to track website traffic, user behavior, and conversion rates. Pay attention to metrics such as page views, bounce rate, and average session duration to understand how users interact with your site.
- **Social Media Analytics**: Platforms like Facebook, Instagram, and Twitter offer built-in analytics to gauge the performance of your posts, including engagement rates, reach, and follower growth. Use this data to refine your social media strategy.
- **Email Marketing Metrics**: Analyze open rates, click-through rates, and conversion rates from your email campaigns to identify what content resonates with your audience and drives action.
- **SEO Performance**: Regularly check your website's ranking for key search terms, the volume of organic traffic, and your backlink profile. Tools such as SEMrush or Moz can provide comprehensive insights into your SEO health.
- **Adjust Based on Insights**: Data should drive your online strategy. Use the insights gained from your analytics to make informed decisions, whether it is tweaking your content strategy, refining your social media approach, or optimizing your email campaigns.

Embracing the Journey of Building Your Online Presence

Building and maintaining a strong online presence is an ongoing journey, not a one-time task. The digital landscape is constantly evolving, with new trends, technologies, and user expectations emerging regularly. Staying adaptable, continuously learning, and being willing to adjust your strategies based on performance data and feedback are key to sustaining success.

Remember, the goal of your online presence is not just visibility but also building meaningful connections with your audience, providing value, and establishing your brand as a trusted authority in your niche. By taking a strategic, data-driven approach to your online presence, as outlined in this chapter, you are well on your way to achieving these objectives.

With patience, persistence, and ongoing engagement, your online presence can become your business's most valuable asset, driving growth and fostering lasting customer relationships.

Chapter 5: Developing Your Product or Service

At the heart of every successful business is a product or service that solves a problem or fulfills a need. Developing your offering is not just about having a good idea; it's about meticulously crafting and refining that idea until it resonates with your target market. This chapter will guide you through the essential stages of product or service development, from understanding customer needs to launching your offering and beyond. With the right approach, you can create a product or service that not only meets but exceeds market expectations, setting the foundation for your business's success.

Understanding Customer Needs

The first step in developing a product or service that sells is understanding what your customers truly need and value. This understanding forms the basis of your offering's design, features, and benefits.

- **Customer Feedback**: Actively seek out feedback from potential and current customers through surveys, interviews, and social media engagement. Listen to their pain points, preferences, and suggestions.
- **Market Research**: Conduct thorough market research to identify trends, gaps, and customer behavior. This research will highlight opportunities for differentiation and innovation in your product or service.
- **Persona Development**: Create detailed buyer personas that represent your ideal customers. These personas should guide your development process, ensuring your offering aligns with the specific needs and desires of your target audience.

Product Development Process

Developing a product involves several stages, from initial concept to market-ready offering. Each stage requires careful planning and execution.

- **Idea Generation**: Start with brainstorming sessions, competitor analysis, and market research to generate viable product ideas.

- **Feasibility Study**: Assess the technical, financial, and market feasibility of your product ideas. This step helps prioritize concepts based on their potential for success.
- **Design and Development**: Begin designing your product, focusing on user experience, functionality, and aesthetics. Prototyping allows you to test and refine your design before full-scale production.
- **Testing**: Conduct extensive testing to ensure your product meets quality standards and customer expectations. This may include beta testing with a select group of customers for real-world feedback.

Service Development and Optimization

Refining Your Service Offering

Creating a compelling service offering requires a focus on customization, scalability, and continuous improvement to meet and exceed customer expectations.

- **Customization and Personalization**: Tailor your services to meet the specific needs of different customer segments. Use customer feedback and data analytics to understand preferences and adapt your services accordingly.
- **Scalability**: Ensure your service model can grow with your business. This might involve automating certain aspects, training additional staff, or expanding your service portfolio.
- **Continuous Improvement**: Establish a feedback loop with your customers to continually refine and improve your services. Consider implementing a versioning system for your services, where you release updates based on customer input and evolving market needs.

Quality Assurance

Ensuring Excellence in Your Offerings

Quality assurance is critical for building trust and loyalty with your customers. It encompasses everything from the initial design to the final delivery of your product or service.

- **Standards and Protocols**: Develop and adhere to high standards and protocols for quality assurance. This might involve industry certifications, regular audits, or adopting best practices in production and delivery.
- **Quality Control Measures**: Implement quality control measures at various stages of the product development or service delivery process. For products, this could include pre-launch testing and post-launch customer feedback. For services, regular training and assessment of service providers ensure consistent quality.
- **Feedback Systems**: Create mechanisms for capturing and analyzing customer feedback. This direct input is invaluable for identifying areas for improvement and enhancing quality.

Pricing Strategies

Setting the Right Price for Your Market

Your pricing strategy is a crucial component of your business model, influencing how your product or service is perceived in the market and directly affecting your profitability.

- **Cost-Based Pricing**: Determine the cost of production or service delivery and add a markup to ensure profitability. This approach is straightforward but must be balanced with market expectations.
- **Value-Based Pricing**: Set your pricing based on the perceived value to the customer rather than just the cost of production. This strategy can support higher price points if your customers believe in the unique benefits or superior quality of your offering.
- **Competitive Analysis**: Consider your competitors' pricing strategies. While you do not have to be the cheapest, understanding the market landscape can help you position your product or service competitively.
- **Dynamic Pricing**: For certain business models, consider dynamic pricing strategies that adjust based on demand, time of year, or customer segment.

Preparing for Product Launch

Launching Your Offering to the Market

The launch phase is critical for introducing your product or service to the market and generating initial interest and sales.

- **Launch Planning**: Develop a comprehensive launch plan that includes target audience identification, marketing and promotional strategies, and logistics for production and distribution.

- **Marketing and Promotion**: Utilize a mix of marketing channels to promote your launch. This could include social media, email marketing, PR, and influencer partnerships. Tailor your messaging to highlight the unique value proposition of your product or service.
- **Monitoring and Adjusting**: Once launched, closely monitor the performance of your product or service. Be prepared to make quick adjustments based on customer feedback and initial sales data. This agility can help you capitalize on momentum and address any issues promptly.

Feedback and Continuous Improvement

Leveraging Customer Feedback for Ongoing Development

After launching your product or service, the journey towards improvement and refinement begins. This continuous loop of feedback and improvement is essential for staying relevant and competitive in the market.

- **Establishing Feedback Channels**: Make it easy for customers to provide feedback through multiple channels, such as online surveys, feedback forms on your website, social media, and direct customer service interactions. Ensure that customers feel their feedback is valued and acted upon.
- **Analyzing Feedback**: Collect and analyze feedback systematically to identify patterns or recurring issues. This analysis can highlight areas for immediate improvement and opportunities for new features or services.
- **Iterative Development**: Adopt an iterative approach to product or service development. Based on customer feedback, prioritize updates and enhancements that will deliver the most value to your customers. This process might involve releasing new versions of a product or making incremental improvements to a service.
- **Communication Improvements**: Keep your customers informed about how their feedback has been implemented. Transparent communication about improvements and updates demonstrates your commitment to customer satisfaction and can enhance loyalty and trust in your brand.

The Path Forward

Developing your product or service is a dynamic and ongoing process that does not end with the launch. The most successful businesses are those that listen to their customers, adapt to changing market demands, and continuously strive for excellence in their offerings. By embracing feedback and making continuous improvement a core part of your business strategy, you can ensure that your product or service not only meets but exceeds customer expectations.

Remember, the development of your product or service is at the heart of what you do. It is the value you provide to your customers, and it is what sets you apart in the marketplace. Keep pushing the boundaries, stay responsive to your customers, and always be prepared to evolve. This is the key to long-term success and growth in today's fast-paced business world.

Chapter 6: Marketing Strategies

I n the digital age, a well-crafted marketing strategy is not just beneficial—it is
essential for the survival and growth of your online business. Marketing
extends your reach, engages your audience, and converts interest into action. This
chapter delves into the core aspects of developing and implementing a marketing
plan that resonates with your target audience and aligns with your business
objectives. From understanding your market to choosing the right channels and
measuring success, we will guide you through creating a marketing strategy that
not only captures attention but also drives results.

Understanding Your Market

Before you can effectively market your product or service, you need a deep
understanding of your market. This means knowing who your customers are,
what they need, and how they make purchasing decisions.

- **Market Research**: Utilize both primary and secondary research to
  gather insights about your target audience. Surveys, interviews, and
  analysis of industry reports can provide valuable information.
- **Customer Personas**: Create detailed personas for your ideal
  customers. Include demographic information, interests, pain points,
  and buying behaviors to tailor your marketing strategies effectively.
- **Competitive Analysis**: Analyze your competitors' marketing
  strategies to identify opportunities. Understanding what works for
  them can provide insights into what might work for you, as well as
  areas where you can differentiate.

Crafting Your Marketing Plan

A strategic marketing plan serves as a roadmap for all your marketing activities.
It ensures that your efforts are aligned with your business goals and provides a
framework for achieving them.

- **Marketing Objectives**: Define clear, measurable objectives.
  Whether it is increasing website traffic, generating leads, or boosting

sales, your goals should be specific and time-bound.

- **Target Audience**: Refine your focus on the target audience identified during your market research. Tailoring your marketing plan to the needs and preferences of this group increases the likelihood of success.
- **Budget**: Determine your marketing budget. A well-defined budget helps allocate resources efficiently across different channels and campaigns.

Digital Marketing Channels

Maximizing Online Visibility Through Diverse Channels

Digital marketing encompasses a range of channels, each with its unique strengths and audience. Selecting the right mix can amplify your reach and engagement.

- **Search Engine Optimization (SEO)**: Focus on optimizing your website and content to rank higher in search engine results, making it easier for potential customers to find you.
- **Pay-Per-Click (PPC) Advertising**: Utilize PPC campaigns through Google Ads or social media platforms to drive targeted traffic to your website. This method allows for precise audience targeting and budget control.
- **Social Media**: Engage with your audience where they spend their time. Each platform serves different purposes and demographics, from the visual appeal of Instagram to the conversational nature of Twitter.
- **Email Marketing**: A direct channel to reach and nurture leads and existing customers. Personalized emails can promote products, share news, and provide value to your audience.
- **Content Marketing**: Attract and retain customers by creating and distributing valuable, relevant content. This approach builds brand authority and keeps your audience engaged over time.

Content Marketing

Engaging Your Audience with Valuable Content

Content marketing is a strategic approach focused on creating and distributing valuable, relevant, and consistent content to attract and retain a clearly defined audience.

- **Content Strategy**: Develop a content strategy that aligns with your marketing goals and speaks directly to your customer's interests and needs. This could include blog posts, videos, infographics, and more.
- **Content Creation**: Produce high-quality content that educates, entertains, or solves problems for your audience. Consistency in tone and message helps build your brand's voice and authority.
- **Distribution and Promotion**: Share your content across your chosen digital marketing channels. Utilize SEO practices, social media, email newsletters, and other platforms to maximize reach.

Social Media Marketing

Building Brand Awareness and Engagement on Social Media

Social media marketing is a powerful tool for businesses to reach their audience, engage with customers, and build brand loyalty.

- **Platform Selection**: Choose platforms that best match your target audience's preferences and behavior. Focus your efforts where you can achieve the highest engagement.
- **Content Planning**: Plan your social media content to reflect your brand's identity and values. A mix of promotional, educational, and interactive content can engage different segments of your audience.
- **Community Engagement**: Actively engage with your followers through comments, messages, and posts. Community management builds relationships and encourages loyalty.

- **Analytics**: Use social media analytics tools to track engagement, reach, and conversion. This data informs your strategy and helps you adjust for better results.

Email Marketing

Nurturing Leads and Customers with Targeted Emails

Email marketing remains one of the most effective ways to communicate directly with your audience, offering exceptional ROI and engagement.

- **List Building**: Grow your email list organically through sign-ups on your website, offering incentives such as discounts or valuable content in exchange for email addresses.
- **Segmentation**: Segment your email list based on customer behavior, preferences, or demographics to send more targeted and relevant messages.
- **Campaigns**: Design email campaigns that nurture leads along the buyer's journey. From welcome emails to promotional blasts and informative newsletters, each email should offer value and encourage action.
- **Compliance and Optimization**: Ensure your email marketing practices comply with regulations like GDPR. Use A/B testing to refine subject lines, content, and calls to action for higher open and conversion rates.

Analyzing and Optimizing Your Marketing Efforts

Making Data-Driven Decisions for Marketing Success

The digital landscape offers a wealth of data to inform and refine your marketing strategies. Continuous analysis and optimization ensure your efforts yield the best possible return on investment (ROI).

- **Analytics Tools**: Utilize tools like Google Analytics, social media insights, and email marketing software to track the performance of your campaigns. These tools provide valuable data on user behavior, engagement rates, conversion rates, and more.

- **Key Performance Indicators (KPIs)**: Identify the KPIs that matter most to your business objectives. This could include website traffic, lead generation numbers, conversion rates, or social media engagement metrics. Monitoring these KPIs helps gauge the success of your marketing strategies.

- **A/B Testing**: Implement A/B testing across your marketing channels to optimize performance. This can involve testing different versions of a webpage, email subject lines, or social media ads to see which performs better.

- **Feedback Loops**: Create feedback loops that allow you to learn from your analytics and apply those insights to future campaigns. This could mean adjusting your content strategy, refining your target audience, or reallocating your budget to more effective channels.

- **Competitive Analysis**: Keep an eye on your competitors' marketing activities. Analyzing their strategies can offer insights and opportunities to differentiate your brand or capitalize on areas they may be overlooking.

Evolving Your Marketing Strategies for Long-Term Growth

Marketing is not a set-it-and-forget-it component of your business. It is a dynamic, ongoing process that requires attention, creativity, and adaptability. As your business grows and the digital landscape changes, so too should your marketing strategies.

- **Stay Informed**: Keep up with the latest trends in digital marketing and your industry. New platforms, tools, and consumer behaviors can offer opportunities for innovation and growth.
- **Customer-Centric Approach**: Always place your customer at the center of your marketing efforts. Understanding their evolving needs and preferences will guide you in creating effective, impactful strategies.
- **Agility**: Be prepared to pivot your strategies based on performance data and market changes. The ability to respond quickly to new information or trends can give you a competitive edge.
- **Continuous Learning**: Consider every campaign an opportunity to learn. Whether a particular strategy was a resounding success or did not perform as expected, there are always insights to be gained that can inform your future efforts.

Chapter 7: Sales and Conversion Tactics

In the digital marketplace, generating traffic and interest is only half the battle; real success lies in converting that interest into sales. This chapter dives into the art and science of sales and conversion tactics, offering strategies to not only capture leads but effectively convert them into paying customers. From crafting a compelling value proposition to optimizing your online presence for conversions, we'll explore the tools and techniques that can enhance your sales process and boost your bottom line.

Understanding the Sales Funnel

The sales funnel is a model that represents the customer journey from initial awareness to the final purchase. Understanding the stages of your sales funnel is crucial for developing targeted strategies that guide potential customers toward making a purchase.

- **Stages of the Sales Funnel**: Break down the funnel into stages—awareness, interest, decision, and action—and tailor your tactics to each phase.
- **Identifying Opportunities**: Analyze your funnel to identify where prospects drop off and implement targeted interventions to improve conversion at each stage.

Crafting Your Value Proposition

Your value proposition is the core reason why customers should choose your product or service over competitors. It encapsulates the unique benefits and features that set your offering apart.

- **Developing a Strong Value Proposition**: Focus on clarity and specificity. Highlight the problems you solve and the benefits you offer that directly address the needs and desires of your target audience.
- **Communicating Value**: Integrate your value proposition into all aspects of your marketing and sales materials, from your website homepage to your social media profiles. Ensure it clearly communicates

the unique benefits your business offers, making it the core message that resonates with your audience. This consistency not only reinforces your brand identity but also helps to attract and retain customers who are looking for what you specifically offer.

Optimizing Your Website for Conversions

Maximizing Website Effectiveness for Higher Sales

Your website serves as the digital storefront for your business, making its optimization crucial for converting visitors into customers.

- **User Experience (UX) Optimization**: Ensure your website offers a seamless, intuitive user experience. Simplify navigation, speed upload times, and make sure it is mobile-friendly to cater to users on all devices.
- **Clear Calls to Action (CTA)**: Use compelling CTAs that guide visitors towards taking the desired action, whether it is making a purchase, signing up for a newsletter, or contacting your business. CTAs should be visible and persuasive, encouraging users to move to the next step.
- **Landing Page Optimization**: Create targeted landing pages for different audiences or campaigns. Each page should focus on a single action or message, minimizing distractions and aligning closely with the users' intentions.
- **A/B Testing**: Regularly test different elements of your website, from headlines and images to CTA buttons and page layouts, to identify what works best at converting visitors.

Leveraging Social Proof

Building Trust and Credibility with Prospective Customers

Social proof can significantly impact your conversion rates by showcasing the satisfaction and success of your current customers.

- **Customer Testimonials and Reviews**: Feature positive testimonials and reviews prominently on your website and sales pages.

Real customer experiences can help alleviate concerns and build trust with potential buyers.

- **Case Studies**: Publish detailed case studies that demonstrate how your product or service solved specific problems for customers. Case studies provide tangible evidence of your value proposition in action.
- **User-Generated Content**: Encourage and share content created by your customers, such as social media posts, unboxing videos, or blog posts. User-generated content adds a level of authenticity and relatability to your brand.

Email Marketing for Sales Conversion

Nurturing Leads Through Personalized Communication

Email marketing remains one of the most effective tools for guiding potential customers through the sales funnel to conversion.

- **Segmentation and Personalization**: Segment your email list based on user behavior, interests, or demographics to send more targeted and relevant communications. Personalized emails can significantly increase engagement and conversion rates.
- **Drip Campaigns**: Implement drip email campaigns that automatically send a series of messages based on specific triggers, such as signing up for a list or abandoning a cart. These campaigns can keep your brand top of mind and gently guide leads towards making a purchase.
- **Value-Driven Content**: Ensure your emails offer value beyond sales pitches. Include useful information, exclusive offers, or engaging content that encourages recipients to stay subscribed and interact with your brand.

Follow-Up Strategies and Customer Retention

Securing Sales and Ensuring Long-Term Loyalty

The follow-up phase is critical not only for closing sales but also for laying the groundwork for long-term customer relationships.

- **Effective Follow-Up Techniques**: Implement a systematic approach for following up with leads. Use a mix of communication channels such as email, phone calls, and social media messages to remind prospects of their interest and address any remaining concerns.
- **Timing and Frequency**: Timing is key in follow-up communications. Too soon, and you might seem pushy; too late, and the lead may cool off. Find the right balance and schedule follow-ups based on lead behavior and preferences.
- **Customer Retention Programs**: Develop programs aimed at retaining customers post-purchase. Loyalty programs, exclusive offers, and regular engagement can encourage repeat business and turn customers into brand advocates.
- **After-Sales Service**: Excellent after-sales service is crucial for retention. Ensure customers are satisfied with their purchase by offering support, tutorials, or helpful resources. A satisfied customer is more likely to return and recommend your business to others.

Measuring and Analyzing Conversion Data

Utilizing Data to Refine and Enhance Sales Strategies

Data analysis plays a pivotal role in understanding the effectiveness of your sales and conversion tactics and identifying areas for improvement.

- **Conversion Tracking**: Utilize tools like Google Analytics to track conversions and important metrics across your website and sales funnel. Monitor everything from page views and bounce rates to specific actions like form submissions or purchases.
- **Customer Journey Analysis**: Map out and analyze the customer

journey to identify bottlenecks or drop-off points where prospects disengage. This insight can help refine your marketing and sales strategies to better guide prospects towards conversion.

- **ROI Calculation**: Calculate the return on investment (ROI) for your marketing and sales activities. Understanding which tactics yield the highest ROI can inform budget allocation and strategy prioritization.
- **A/B Testing Results**: Continuously test and compare different elements of your sales process, from email subject lines to landing page designs. Use the data from these tests to make informed decisions about what changes to implement for improved performance.

Adapting and Evolving Your Conversion Tactics for Business Growth

The landscape of online sales and marketing is ever-evolving, and so too should be your approach to sales and conversion tactics. Staying informed about new trends, technologies, and consumer behaviors is essential for maintaining and enhancing your competitive edge.

- **Commitment to Continuous Improvement**: The key to sustained growth is a commitment to continuously testing, learning, and optimizing your sales strategies based on data and feedback.
- **Customer-Centric Focus**: Always keep the needs and preferences of your customer at the forefront of your sales and conversion efforts. A deep understanding of your target audience will guide more effective and impactful strategies.
- **Flexibility and Resilience**: Be prepared to adapt your tactics in response to market changes, new competitors, or shifts in consumer behavior. Flexibility and resilience are crucial qualities in the fast-paced digital marketplace.

Chapter 8: Scaling Your Business

S caling your business is a journey that extends beyond initial success, requiring careful planning, strategic investment, and a focus on long-term sustainability. This chapter explores the multifaceted process of scaling, from assessing your readiness to leveraging technology and expanding your market presence. With the right approach, scaling can propel your business to new heights, unlocking opportunities for increased revenue, market share, and impact.

Assessing Readiness for Scaling

Before embarking on expansion, it is crucial to assess whether your business is truly ready to scale. This involves evaluating your current operations, market demand, and financial health.

- **Operational Stability**: Is your business running smoothly, with efficient processes and a solid customer base? Operational gaps can become magnified during scaling.
- **Market Demand**: Do market research to confirm that demand is likely to grow or sustain with your expanded offerings or geographic reach.
- **Financial Health**: Ensure you have steady revenue streams and healthy profit margins. Scaling often requires significant investment before additional revenue is realized.

Developing a Scalable Business Model

A scalable business model is key to successful growth. It should allow for increased revenue without a corresponding increase in costs.

- **Automation and Standardization**: Identify processes that can be automated or standardized to reduce manual effort and costs as you grow.
- **Flexible Offerings**: Consider how your products or services can be

adapted or expanded to meet broader customer needs or tap into new markets.

- **Revenue Streams**. Diversify your revenue streams to ensure stability. This might include adding subscription models, licensing, or ancillary services.

Financing Growth

Securing the Funds to Fuel Your Expansion

Growth often requires capital. Choosing the right financing option can determine how effectively you can scale.

- **Venture Capital (VC)**: For businesses with high growth potential, venture capital can provide significant funding. However, it often requires giving up equity and some level of control.
- **Loans and Lines of Credit**: Traditional bank loans or lines of credit offer a debt financing route. They are suitable for businesses with solid credit histories and predictable revenue streams.
- **Crowdfunding**: Platforms like Kickstarter or Indiegogo can be excellent for product-based businesses looking to gauge market interest and raise funds without giving up equity.
- **Bootstrapping and Internal Cash Flow**: Reinvesting profits back into the business is a conservative approach to scaling and maintaining control but potentially limiting the speed of growth.

Expanding Your Product or Service Line

Diversifying Offerings to Capture More Market Share

Introducing new products or services can attract different customer segments and increase revenue.

- **Market Research**: Validate new ideas with thorough market research to ensure there's demand.
- **Customer Feedback**: Leverage existing customer feedback to identify opportunities for new offerings that complement your current lineup.
- **Innovation**: Stay ahead of market trends and consider how emerging

technologies or shifts in consumer behavior could influence your product development.

Exploring New Markets

Reaching Beyond Your Current Audience

Expanding into new geographic or demographic markets can significantly increase your customer base.

- **Market Analysis**: Conduct detailed analysis to identify markets with unmet needs that your business can fulfill. Consider cultural, economic, and regulatory factors.
- **Localization**: Adapt your marketing, sales strategies, and possibly your offerings to meet local tastes and compliance requirements.
- **Partnerships**: Collaborate with local businesses or influencers to gain market insights and facilitate entry into new markets.

Leveraging Technology for Efficiency and Growth

Using Tech to Scale Operations and Enhance Customer Experience

Technology can streamline operations, improve customer service, and support data-driven decision-making.

- **Automation Tools**: Implement tools for automating repetitive tasks in areas like customer service, marketing, and inventory management.
- **Customer Relationship Management (CRM)**: A robust CRM system can help manage growing customer data and personalize interactions at scale.
- **Data Analytics**: Utilize analytics to gain insights into customer behavior, operational efficiency, and market opportunities.

Building a Team to Support Growth

Cultivating a Workforce That Grows With Your Business

As your business scales, so does the need for a skilled and adaptable team that can drive and support this growth.

- **Strategic Hiring**: Focus on hiring individuals not just for current roles but for their potential to take on greater responsibilities as the business evolves. Look for adaptability, cultural fit, and a growth mindset.
- **Leadership Development**: Invest in training and development programs to cultivate leadership skills among your team members. Effective leadership is crucial for managing larger teams and new business challenges.
- **Culture and Engagement**: Maintain a strong company culture that supports engagement and retention. As your team grows, clear communication of your mission, values, and expectations will help preserve the essence of what makes your business unique.

Tracking Growth and Navigating Challenges

With growth comes the need to measure success accurately and manage the risks associated with scaling.

- **Growth Metrics**: Identify key performance indicators (KPIs) that accurately reflect the health and growth of your business. These might include revenue growth rate, customer acquisition cost, customer lifetime value, and net promoter score (NPS).
- **Risk Management**: Scaling introduces new risks, from operational challenges to financial uncertainties. Implement risk management strategies, including diversification, financial reserves, and continuous market analysis, to mitigate these risks.

- **Quality Control**: Ensure that your commitment to quality does not waver as you scale. Implement systems and checks to maintain product or service standards, customer satisfaction, and brand reputation.

Embracing Strategic Growth for Long-Term Success

Scaling your business is an exciting journey that requires careful planning, strategic investment, and a focus on sustainable practices. By assessing your readiness to scale, developing a scalable business model, and strategically navigating financing, market expansion, and technology integration, you can set your business on a path to successful growth.

Chapter 9: Managing Challenges

Embarking on an entrepreneurial journey is akin to navigating a sea of constant change. Challenges, both expected and unforeseen, are inevitable milestones along this path. This chapter doesn't just acknowledge these obstacles; it aims to arm you with resilience and strategic foresight. You'll learn not only to anticipate challenges but also to transform them into opportunities for growth and innovation.

Identifying Potential Challenges

The digital landscape is ever-evolving, marked by rapid market saturation, technological disruptions, and shifts in consumer behavior. Understanding these dynamics is crucial for any online business.

- **Forecasting Tools**: Leverage analytical tools and market trend reports to stay ahead of industry shifts. Utilizing platforms like Google Trends and conducting SWOT analyses can provide foresight into potential challenges.
- **Strategic Planning**: Develop a flexible business strategy that includes contingency plans for various scenarios. Regularly updating your business plan based on market feedback and forecasts helps in navigating through turbulent times.

Financial Management and Cash Flow Issues

A robust financial foundation is critical for weathering the storms of business uncertainties.

- **Cash Flow Management**: Implement rigorous budgeting practices and maintain a liquidity reserve to manage cash flow effectively. Tools like QuickBooks or Xero can provide valuable insights into your financial health.

- **Risk Mitigation**: Diversify income sources and consider various financing options, such as lines of credit or angel investment, to safeguard against financial crunches.

Navigating Market Changes

Staying relevant in a rapidly changing market requires agility and an unwavering focus on customer needs.

- **Market Adaptability**: Embrace a culture of continuous innovation within your organization. Use customer feedback loops and market research to guide your product development and marketing strategies.
- **Pivoting Strategies**: Be prepared to pivot your business model in response to significant market shifts. Success stories of companies that have successfully pivoted can serve as inspiration and guidance.

Dealing with Competition

In a crowded online marketplace, standing out from the competition is both a challenge and a necessity.

- **Unique Value Proposition (UVP)**: Clearly define and communicate your UVP. It's essential for differentiating your business and attracting your target audience.
- **Competitive Analysis**: Regularly conduct competitive analyses to understand your competitors' strengths and weaknesses. Tools like SEMrush and Ahrefs can offer insights into their strategies and performance.

Technological Challenges and Solutions

Technology is a double-edged sword—offering opportunities for growth while posing potential threats.

- **Adopting New Technologies**: Stay informed about emerging technologies relevant to your industry. Participate in webinars, conferences, and professional networks to learn about tools that can enhance your business operations.

- **Cybersecurity Measures**: Invest in robust cybersecurity measures to protect your business and customer data. Regular training for your team on security best practices is also crucial.

Human Resources and Team Dynamics

As your business grows, so does the complexity of managing your team and preserving your company culture.

- **Team Development**: Invest in professional development and team-building activities to maintain a motivated and cohesive team.
- **Conflict Resolution**: Establish clear communication channels and conflict resolution mechanisms to address interpersonal challenges promptly and effectively.

Legal and Regulatory Compliance

The online business environment is subject to various legal and regulatory considerations.

- **Compliance Strategy**: Stay abreast of legal changes affecting your business. Consider engaging legal counsel specializing in digital commerce to navigate these complexities.
- **Global Considerations**: For businesses operating internationally, understanding and complying with global regulations is paramount. Tools and consultants specialized in international law can be invaluable resources.

Personal Challenges as an Entrepreneur

Managing personal well-being is as crucial as managing your business.

- **Wellness and Balance**: Implement practices that support your mental and physical health. Time management tools and mindfulness techniques can help balance work and life.
- **Continuous Learning**: Embrace a mindset of lifelong learning.

Seek mentorship, attend workshops, and engage with peer networks to support both personal and professional growth.

Challenges in business are not roadblocks but rather catalysts for growth, pushing you to evolve and adapt. With the right strategies, mindset, and support, you can navigate these challenges successfully. Remember, resilience is built through overcoming obstacles, and every challenge overcome is a step forward in your entrepreneurial journey.

Conclusion

In the culmination of our journey through the entrepreneurial landscape, we arrive at a pivotal moment of reflection and anticipation. The path of entrepreneurship is strewn with challenges and triumphs, each a stepping stone towards realizing your vision. As we close this chapter, remember that the essence of entrepreneurship lies not in the avoidance of obstacles but in the resilience and creativity with which you navigate them.

Your journey is uniquely yours, marked by personal aspirations, innovative ideas, and the unwavering pursuit of success. The strategies and insights shared within these pages are tools to guide you, but it is your passion, determination, and adaptability that will carve your path in the business world.

As you stand on the brink of this exciting venture, let the challenges inspire you, the opportunities invigorate you, and the successes, no matter how small, fuel your ambition. The entrepreneurial journey is a continuous learning process, one that demands persistence, evolves with every step, and rewards the courageous.

Now, armed with knowledge and bolstered by a community of fellow entrepreneurs, you are ready to turn your dreams into reality. Begin with a plan, but be prepared to adapt. Embrace innovation, but stay true to your values. Seek growth, but never at the expense of your well-being or that of your team.

The future is not written; it is crafted by those daring enough to venture forth and shape it. Let this be your call to action. Start where you are, use what you have, and do what you can. Your entrepreneurial journey begins now—embrace it with an open heart and a steadfast spirit.

And so, as we part ways in text, remember that the end of this book is not the end but the beginning of your remarkable journey. Go forth with confidence, curiosity, and the courage to transform your vision into a thriving reality. The world awaits the mark you will leave, and it is time to show it what you are made of.

Appendix

R esource List

Market Research Tools

- Google Trends: For understanding search trends and consumer interest.
- Statista: Comprehensive statistics and data for market analysis.
- U.S. Census Bureau: Demographic data for market segmentation.

Financial Management Tools

- QuickBooks: Accounting software for small businesses.
- Mint: Budgeting tool for tracking and managing expenses.
- Wave: Free financial software for small businesses, offering invoicing and accounting features.

Digital Marketing and SEO Tools

- Google Analytics: For tracking website traffic and user behavior.
- SEMrush: SEO and digital marketing research.
- Hootsuite: Social media management platform.

Legal and Regulatory Resources

- LegalZoom: Online legal services and documents.
- U.S. Small Business Administration (SBA): Guides on legal and regulatory compliance for small businesses.
- GDPR.eu: Information on GDPR compliance for businesses operating in or with customers in the EU.

Technology and Productivity Tools

- Slack: Communication tool for teams.

- Trello or Asana: Project management tools.
- Zapier: Automation tool to connect your apps and automate workflows.

Recommended Reading

"The Lean Startup" by Eric Ries: Principles of lean startup methodology for developing businesses and products. **2. "Zero to One" by Peter Thiel**: Insights on innovation, competition, and starting a business. **3. "Building a StoryBrand" by Donald Miller**: Framework for clarifying your brand message and marketing more effectively.

Case Studies

Provide a selection of case studies highlighting successful online businesses that started small and scaled effectively. Include key strategies they employed, challenges faced, and lessons learned.

D. Glossary

Define key terms used throughout the book, such as:

- SEO (Search Engine Optimization)
- PPC (Pay-Per-Click advertising)
- CRM (Customer Relationship Management)

E. Templates and Checklists

1. Business Plan Template: Outline for creating a comprehensive business plan. **2. Marketing Plan Checklist**: Essential components of a digital marketing strategy. **3. Financial Planning Worksheet**: Template for budgeting and financial forecasting.

9 798224 323609